ANTUAN is still HEAR
30 Years of more kids' quotes

ISBN 978-1-948613-21-7
Library of Congress Control Number: 2023908229

Printed in the United States of America

Sunny Day Publishing, LLC
Cuyahoga Falls, Ohio 44223
www.sunnydaypublishing.com
editor@sunnydaypublishing.com

ANTUAN Is still HEAR:
(30 years of more kids' quotes) *

written and Illustrated
by
Irv Korman

* A sequel to "Antuan was Hear:
(30 Years of Kids' quotes)"
(2016)

Book cover design by Melanie Korman

This book is dedicated to:

Stanley H.
Michael M.
Betsy R.
Andre S.
and
Antuan D.

FORWARD

In 2016, my fourth book was published, titled, "Antuan was Hear: (30 Years of Kids' Quotes)."

From 1967 to 1997, I was employed by The Akron Public Schools located in my hometown of Akron, Ohio.

I was a speech/language therapist assigned to elementary school buildings.

After identifying the speech/language problem and securing parent permission, I scheduled groups of about five students per group for a one half-hour session two times a week. Most of the sessions consisted of correcting consonant mispronunciations of age-appropriate consonant sounds. To make it a simple explanation: the students' speech problems sounded a lot like Warner Brothers cartoon characters mispronunciations of (s), (l), (r), (th) and a few other consonant sounds and their blends with other consonants and/or vowels. Yes, some of my students sounded like Elmer Fudd, Sylvester the Cat, Tweetie Bird, Daffy Duck, and Porky Pig.

During the therapy sessions, to take the students' minds off their task, I would ask them non-speech therapy questions to see if their corrected target sound carried over into their daily speech and language patterns.

From the beginning, some of the students' statements and comments were so funny to me that I would momentarily stop the speech therapy session to quickly jot down the quote in the back of my lesson plan book.

What was so funny to me, was how serious the students were in their innocent verbal responses.

When I finally retired, I found my thirty lesson plan books and began laughing and recalling the clever utterances of my young students.

I then began the arduous task of transferring each individual student quotation from the back of all my lesson plan books onto a 3 X 5 index card; one quote for each card.

After a flood in my basement, I found the box containing my lesson plan books with my students' quotes and index cards. It was unharmed by the flood.

I approached Sunny Day Publishing with the idea of a sequel to "Antuan Was Hear: (30 Years of Kids' Quotes)" using the unused quotes on the remaining nearly 300 index cards.

The result is the official sequel to "Antuan Was Hear: (30 Years of Kids' Quotes)."

If you are wondering how I came to select the title for the book, I have included the original 2016 "Preface" to it. The story of how I came across the quote for the book title is worth reading.

Sadly, Antuan has passed away. Every time I hear a humorous quote from a child, even today, I still think of Antuan.

Rest in Peace, dear Antuan.

Preface from 2016 published book of "Antuan Was Hear: (30 Years of Kids' Quotes)"

There are probably not very many millionaire teachers. At least I have never heard about or met any. Most teachers must find other ways to supplement their teaching income.

For 30 years (1978 to 2008) I had the good fortune of being a freelance entertainment writer for several monthly, weekly, and daily publications in Northeastern Ohio to supplement my teaching income.

Juggling teaching and interviewing celebrities can be tricky at times. One such situation resulted in the title of this book "Antuan Was Hear: (30 Years of Kids' Quotes)."

In the spring of 1996, I had arranged to interview Bob Keeshan, aka Captain Kangaroo of children's television fame. I had interviewed him once before, in May of 1987. He appeared in Akron (Ohio) at the behest of Akron Children's Medical Center, lecturing as a child advocate. The spring of 1996, opportunity arose to interview him, again, this time before appearing at a local book store (Borders) to promote one of his latest children's books, "Alligator In the Basement."

As previously stated, juggling teaching with daytime phone interviews can be tricky. I had arranged with Keeshan's publicity agent to interview him during my lunch period from my home. It would give me time to drive to my home, set up my tape recorder, call Keeshan and interview him before leaving home and going to my next scheduled school in the afternoon. As an elementary school speech/language pathologist it was my practice to be at one school building in the morning, and different school in the afternoon.

I gave Keeshan's agent my AM school phone number just in case there was any last-minute change. The agent and Keeshan must have misunderstood my message because midway through an AM speech therapy group session, the school secretary paged me over the entire school's public address system: "Mr. Korman, please come to the office. Captain Kangaroo is on the phone."

You can imagine the school faculty's reaction to the message. To this day I still get reminded of the event many, many years after it happened. I dismissed my speech session and went to the school office. Bob Keeshan was on the phone, ready for his scheduled interview. I informed him there must have been a miscommunication because I was not scheduled to interview him until 12: 00 noon from my home. I explained the situation to Keeshan and he understood. He said he would call me at 12 noon at my home phone number.

I don't recall how much time passed between the speech therapy session I dismissed to take the phone call and my next scheduled session. I hurried back to my room to find it was passed the time for the next scheduled session. It was obvious to me that one of the next scheduled students had come to the room at the correct time and found the room quite empty. To let me know he did show up for his appropriate session time the student left the following note printed in chalk on the speech room's chalkboard:

"Antuan Was Hear."

Author's note: Sometimes, in writing an original quote down, I would later go back to read it and realize I forgot the student's name. On the following pages, quotes from forgotten names are labeled "student." When a student's name is used, it's most likely not the originator of the quote, so as "to protect the name(s) of the innocent."

HOLIDAYS and SEASONS

—Halloween—

Teacher: How much candy did you get on Beggar's Night for Halloween?
Student: I got almost a whole half bag full!

Teacher: Students, what costumes did you see on Halloween?
Student #1: Someone in a married costume.
Student #2: Someone wrapped in rags. He was a mommy.
Student #3: A stuffed man.
Student #4: A lady that was a boy.
Student #5: One kid dressed up as Laurel and Hardy.
Student #6: One girl was Little Miss Muffin.

Teacher: What are you going to be for Halloween?
Student: My cousin gonna buy us some invisible paint and paint us invisible!

Teacher: What were you for Halloween?
Student #1: Soul Brother Superman.
Student #2: A pimp.
Student #3: A dead prom queen.

Teacher: What did some people you saw dress up as for Halloween?
Student: Greg was Charlie Brown but he didn't look it.
Teacher: Then how did you know he was Charlie Brown?
Student: He told me.

Teacher: Are you having a Halloween Party?
Student: Yes.
Teacher: What kind?
Student: A birthday party!

Teacher: John, what do you do on Halloween?
John: Celebrate my grandma's birthday!

Teacher: What did you dress up as for Halloween?
Student: A football.

Teacher: What were you for Halloween?
Student: A robot and a hippie.
Teacher: How could you be both?
Student: I was a hippie under the robot outfit!

Teacher: What did you wear to your Halloween party at school?
Student: Nothin'. I forgot my sheet!

Teacher (to a boy student): What are you going to dress up as for Halloween?
Boy student: A girl.
Teacher (to a girl student): What are you going to dress up as for Halloween?
Girl student: A boy.

Teacher: Adam, what did some teachers dress up for Halloween?
Adam: Mrs. Sanders was dressed up like nothing.

Teacher: Stacey, what did you do for Halloween?
Stacey: I went to a hunted house.

Teacher: Corey, what do you call a pumpkin when it is carved with a scary face?
Corey: A Jack-o-Lemon!

Britney: Know what, teacher? My brother is gonna be a headless ghost without a head!

—Thanksgiving—

Teacher: For Thanksgiving, what is your favorite part of the turkey?
Student #1: The chicken leg.
Student #2: The feathers.
Student #3: The meat!

Teacher: What did you do over Thanksgiving?
Student #1: I peeked in the turkey.
Student #2: I watched the football game on television between the Detroit Lions and the Kansas Sissy Chiefs.

Student: Teacher, over Thanksgiving I fell down.
Teacher: What else did you do?
Student: I got up!

Student: Teacher, do you know why Santa Claus waits till after Thanksgiving to come out?
Teacher: No. Why?
Student: So he can show everyone how fat he got over Thanksgiving!

Teacher: Do you know the story about Thanksgiving?
Student: Isn't it about William Tell?

Teacher: What is in your classroom for Thanksgiving?
Student: Some fruit and a picture of God.

Carl: On Thanksgiving I didn't have turkey. I had food!

Student: I can hardly wait till Thanksgiving 'cause we're havin' a 16 foot turkey!

Teacher: What did you have to eat on Thanksgiving?
Michael: We had dead turkey and smashed potatoes.

—CHRISTMAS—

Teacher: What did you get for Christmas?
Student #1: A gee-tire!
Student #2: A stomach ache.
Robert: I got three polo shirts from Lax Fifth Avenue.

Teacher: What did you get for Christmas?
Student: I got $27.00. But I only got to
keep $7.00 of it.
Teacher: Then your mother put the rest in
the bank. Right?
Student: No. She kept it.

Teacher: What did you do over Christmas
Vacation?
Student #1: My aunt came down and fell in
the snow.
Student: #2: I earned money shoveling
walks, porches, driveways and swimming
pools.
Student #3: We were going to Florida but
my dad forgot.

Teacher: What did you do over Christmas
Vacation?
Student: Play with my football and race
car set.
Teacher: And what did you get for
Christmas?
Student: A football and race car set.

Teacher: And what did you do over Christmas vacation?
Student #1: I'm not Christian so I didn't do much.
Student #2 (to Student #1): Oh, then you must have had a Charlie Brown Christmas!

Lanette: I don't believe in Santa Claus.
Teacher: Then, Lanette, who is that jolly man at the mall in a red suit wearing a beard?
Lanette: A stranger.

Teacher: Name some of Santa's reindeer.
Student: Dancer, Prancer, and Cancer.

Erica: I was gonna bring you a present but my mom wouldn't let me.

James: I got you a Christmas present but I left it at home.

Wesley: I don't believe in Santa Claus. Anyway, when he comes down the chimney it's like breaking in!

Student: One day Christmas will be gone.

—Easter—

Teacher: What did you do over Easter Vacation?
Student: I went out in the rain and came in with water on.

Teacher: Did you go to church for Easter?
Student: Yes. With my mother.
Teacher: Did your mother wear an Easter bonnet?
Student: No.
Teacher: What then?
Student: She wore a hat!

Teacher: Lamar, what did the Easter Bunny leave?
Lamar: Malted mothballs!

—Valentine's Day—

Teacher: Mary, how was your Valentine's Day?
Mary: I had to go to the dentist.
Teacher: Don't feel bad, Mary. It takes a long time to get a dental appointment. Ideally you should go to the dentist twice a year.
Robby: I don't! I go every six months!

—Mother's Day—

Teacher: What are you getting your mother for Mother's Day?
Bryan: We makin' Valentines!
Carol: Roses. I stole 'em.
Lamar: Pot.
Donna: She don't have any rings but I got her a ring box.
Derek: I'm gonna give my mom a look!
Steve: Two packs of cigarettes and Excedrin.
Gerald: I'm going to take my mom to a beer joint.
Thomas: I'm gonna borrow some money from my mom and buy her a pizza.
Damon: I am going to buy her a beer.
Elizabeth: A coffee pot. She hates coffee.

Sheila: I already got my mom a Mother's Day present.
Teacher: Why? It's two days before Mother's Day.
Sheila: Because it broke.

Teacher: What happened on Mother's Day?
Melissa: My mom had a nervous wreck.

Teacher: How is your mother?
Student: Nothing is wrong with her!

—Fall/Autumn—

Teacher: what do we do in autumn after the leaves turn color and fall to the ground?
Daniel: we shovel them into piles.

Student: I got a job shovelin' leaves!

I got a great idea: Let's build a snowball!

—Winter—

Teacher: It's snowing outside. What can you do in the snow?
Student: Get the flu!

Teacher: What do you like to do in the winter?
Student: Build a snowball.

In winter
too Keep
warm I
wear ear
muffins.

—Spring—

Teacher: What do you have when the weather is warm and you can eat outside?
Michael: A pigment!

Teacher: What happens in the spring?
Darrell: A tomato storm!

Teacher: What do you have in your classroom that reminds you of spring?
Student: Open windows.

Aaron: My birthday is in spring and summer.

Teacher: What is your favorite season?
Student: Summer.
Teacher: Why?
Student: 'Cause when it's hot you can go inside and get cool. But if it's cold you can't get hot again.

—Memorial Day—

Teacher: What are you going to do on Memorial Day?
Brenda: I'm gonna wear green.
Teacher: What are you doing over Memorial Day?
Student: I'm going camping.
Teacher: With your family?
Student: No. With my family.

—GEORGE WASHINGTON'S BIRTHDAY—

Anthony: We learned about George Washington.
Teacher: What did you learn about him?
Anthony: He was born.

Teacher: Who was George Washington?
Student: I got a book about him at home.
Teacher: Tell me about him.
Student: I can't.
Teacher: Why not?
Student: I haven't read the book yet.

Teacher: Who was George Washington?
Student: A famous man.
Teacher: What did he do to become famous?
Student: He died.

Teacher: Who was George Washington?
Student: He was our first President in 1929.

Teacher: Who was George Washington?
Student: A President.
Teacher: What did he do?
Student: Chopped down a cherry tree.
Teacher: After he did what did his father do?
Student: He died.

Teacher: What did George Washington do?
Student: Chopped down a cherry tree.
Teacher: Why?
Student: To get a whooppin'.

Teacher: Why did George Washington chop down a cherry tree?
Student: It was old.

Teacher: Who was George Washington?
Student: Father of our country.
Teacher: What did he do?
Student: Stood up in a boat.

Teacher: Who was George Washington?
Student: He chopped down the first cherry tree.

Teacher: Who was George Washington?
Student: He chopped down a cherry tree.
Teacher: What happened when he chopped it down?
Student: His father came out.
Teacher: Then what happened to him?
Student: He crossed the Delaware.

Teacher: Who can tell me who George Washington was?
Student: He led the war.
Teacher: Which one?
Student: Two.

Teacher: Who was George Washington?
Student: President.
Teacher: Of what?
Student: The United States.
Teacher: What else did he do?
Student: He was in the war.
Teacher: Which one?
Student: Both.

Teacher: Who was George Washington?
Student: He discovered America.

Teacher: Who was President before Richard Nixon?
Student: George Washington.

Teacher: Name a famous person.
Student: George Washington, D.C.

Teacher: George Washington's home was
called Mount...
Aaron: Everest!

(Akron Public Schools had a special day
when students brought clothes to donate
to Goodwill. It was called "Goodwill Bundle
Day")

Teacher: Who can tell me what GWBD
stands for?
Student: George Washington's Birthday!

Sarah: George Washington died of
ammonia!

—ABRAHAM LINCOLN'S BIRTHDAY—

Teacher: Who was Abe Lincoln?
Student: A President.
Teacher: How do you know?
Student: I made a report on him!

Teacher: Abraham Lincoln had four sons but only one grew up.
Jason: You mean the rest stayed babies?

Teacher: Who was Abe Lincoln?
Student: 16th President.
Teacher: Very good. What did he do as President?
Student: He freezed the slaves.

Teacher: Whose birthday was it last week?
Student: Abe Lincoln. He was the founder of the light bulb.

Teacher: Who was Abraham Lincoln?
Student: He was the 16th President.
Teacher: What else?
Student: He kept his information in his hat. That's why it was so tall.

Teacher: Tell me about Abraham Lincoln.
Donald: He got shot.
David: He got shot at a puppet show.

Teacher: Who was Abraham Lincoln?
Student #1: 16th President.
Student: #2: Is he dead?

Teacher: Who was Abe Lincoln?
Student: He signed a contract to free the slaves.

Teacher: Who can tell me something about Abraham Lincoln?
Student: He was President. He went on a boat and saw the slaves and became President!

Teacher: Who was Abe Lincoln?
Student: A President who got shot in the head at a theater.
Teacher: Who was Abraham Lincoln?
Student: He went to a movie and got shot.

Teacher: Who was Abe Lincoln?
Student: #16th President.
Teacher: What else can you tell us about him?
Student: He chopped down the first cherry tree.

I know where pencils
come from: Pencil —van la

FAMILY and OTHER RELATIVES

Brenda: My mom got sick then she got unsick!

Adam: My brother's grandma died.

Robert: My sister is a spoiled brat!
Teacher: How old is your sister?
Robert: Eight months.

Tammy: Teacher, guess what? My mom and dad are getting married!

Lamar: My cousins are all girls but my brother is a boy.

Teacher: Do you have any brothers or sisters at home?
Student: Yes. I have a sister and a foster baby. It's a brother.

Teacher: Pierre, how old is your baby sister?
Pierre: Zero.

Brandon: I'm going to Columbus this weekend.
Teacher: To visit relatives?
Brandon: No, to see my aunt.

Teacher: What's the matter?
Student: I gotta headache.
Teacher: What from?
Student: Every time my sister sees me she hits me on the head.

Teacher: Finish this sentence for me: "I'll never forget...."
Samantha: "....when my parents got married!"

Teacher: Do you have an older sister or brother?
Student: Brother.
Teacher: Where does he go to school?
Student: The Universery of Akron.

Edward: Did I tell you about my grandma?
Teacher: No.
Edward: She died.

Teacher: Fred, do you like girls?
Fred: No. I like my mother but hate girls.

Lori: Friday we went to see my uncle 'cause he died.

Teacher: How many are in your family?
Student: I got sisters not counting the dog.

Linda: Smell my hair.
Teacher: It smells good. What is it?
Linda: My brother's hair grease!

Student: Everyone loves my mother. My dad loves her and so does a man named Robert.

Student: Know what happened yesterday?
Teacher: No.
Student: My grandpa got buried.

Laconia: You look just like my daddy but he's brown.

Teacher: That's a nice dress you have on. Is it for Easter?
Crystal: No. My dad's getting married!

Teacher: Do you get along with your sister?
Jennifer: I can answer that in two words: "Give me a break!"

Laura: My mom forgot my dad's seventeenth birthday.

Jeremy: I don't have a sister 'cause my mom can't afford one.

Samantha: My sister is in the hospital. She had an operation because she breathes too fast.

Shawn: My brother got a broken eye.

Teacher: Leonard, put "cast" in a sentence.
Leonard: When my daddy died he was put in a "cast."

Anthony: I spent the night at my grandpa's one day.

Karen: My mom called the plumber to fix the television.

Brittany: My dad accidently moved into a house with another woman.

MOVIES and TELEVISION SHOWS

Author's note: These motion pictures and TV shows are from the 1960s through the 1990s.

Teacher: Seen any good movies?
Student: I saw "Spark-tackle-us."

Teacher: Seen a good movie lately?
Student: Yeah: "Florence of Arabia."

Teacher: What movie have you seen lately?
Student: "Franklin-stein."

Brandon: I saw "Snow White and the Seven Drawers!"

Tim: I saw that Big Foot story on "Unsalted Mysteries."

Teacher: what do you like to watch on television?
Martin: "Family Manners"
Student#1: "Michigan Impossible"
Student #2: "The Cornchip of Eddie's Father"
Student #3: "Supperman"
Student #4: "The Red Skeleton Show"
Ed: "The Long Ranger"

Teresa: Joyce Dewitt is going off "Three's Company." She's the one who makes things worth wild.

Student: Wanna buy a TV Guide magazine?
Teacher: What for?
Student: For fifteen cents.

Student: We got a new color television!
Teacher: Really?
Student: Yeah. Now we have two sets: a colored one and an uncolored one.

Teacher: What is the television cartoon show that has little blue people in it?
Student: The Smidgets!

Ben: (about television shows) There are reruns and new runs!

OVER the WEEKEND

Teacher: What did you do over the weekend?
Edward: We went sledding and saw this big dog. I think it was a German Pinscher!
Tanya I played "Hide and Go Seek" by myself.
Robert: I went over to my girlfriend's house and played with her brother.
Derek: I caught a cold.
Matt: I put a snail down my shirt.
David: I went to Seiberling Nature Center and felt a toad.
Marty: My mom bought me a model of a cave.

Teacher: What did you do over the weekend?
Terry: We went to a farewell party for my cousins. They movin' away.
Teacher: Are they moving far away?
Terry: Yes. Somewhere in New York.
Teacher: New York City?
Terry: No. New Jersey.

Teacher: What did you do over the weekend?
Student: We went to North Carolina.
Teacher: Did you visit relatives?
Student: No. Cousins.

Teacher: Adam, what did you do over the weekend?
Adam: I went to Youngstown.
Teacher: Did you visit relatives?
Adam: No, my dad's wife.

Teacher: Wendy, what did you do over the weekend?
Wendy (age 5): Play with my cousin.
Teacher: Oh. How old is he?
Wendy: Forty.

Teacher: What did you do over the weekend?
Student: On Sunday we went to church. We saw my daddy in the sheriff's car!

Teacher: what are you doing over the weekend?

Student: My grandma is taking me to an "option."

Teacher: what is an "option"?

Student: you know, where somebody hold somethin' up and people bid on it.

Teacher: what are doing over the weekend?

Dan: My girlfriend is letting me take her snake for a walk.

Teacher: Darryl, what are you doing over the weekend?

Darryl: we're gonna see Ringling Brothers and Barnaby Circus!

I mixed popcorn kernels in the pancake batter. Now the pancakes can flip themselves over!

ILLNESS

Teacher: I haven't seen you in school for a long time. Where have you been?
Student: I've been sick.
Teacher: What did you have?
Student: A headache and stomach ache.
Teacher: How did you get them?
Student: My sister had them and I caught 'em from her.

Teacher: Adam, you weren't here last week. Were you sick?
Adam: No. I wasn't sick. I had to go to the hospital.

Student: My sister is not in school today.
Teacher: Where is she?
Student: At home.
Teacher: Is she sick?
Student: Yeah.
Teacher: Does she have a cold or something?
Student: No.
Teacher: What then?
Student: The flu.

Teacher: What happened to your ankle?
Student: I hurt it playing football.
Teacher: How?
Student: I fell over a rat hole.
Teacher: That's bad.
Student: Yeah. Especially if the rat's home!

Teacher: Where were you last week?
Student: I was home.
Teacher: Yes, I know. But why? Were you sick?
Student: No.
Teacher: Then why were you at home and not at school?
Student: I had a high fever.

Teacher: Why haven't you been in school lately?
Student: I was sick.
Teacher: What did you have?
Student: Swollen gills.

William: My brother's going in the hospital today for an operation on his feet. When they're done they got him to walk on crunches!

Kris: My brother had stitches in his head. They had to give him ovalcane to numb it first.

Donna: Teacher, there's a girl in our class who keeps falling down!
Sabrina: Yeah, she keeps having Caesars!

Michael: I was in the office this morning.
Teacher: Why?
Michael: I was too hyper.

Teacher: You've been absent for a few days. Were you sick?
Student: No.
Teacher. Oh.
Student: I went to the doctor.

OCCUPATIONS

Teacher: What do you want to be when you grow up?
Student: A fireman.
Teacher: If you were a fireman, what would you do?
Student: Put out houses!

Teacher: What do you want to be when you grow up?
Student: My momma tells me I want to be a stewardess. But I want to be a nurse.

Robert: My brother got a job!
Teacher: Doing what?
Robert: He's a waitress at The Egg Castle Restaurant!

GEOGRAPHY

Teacher: What countries were represented in your May Festival Songfest?
Student: Ohio, and I think Europe.

Teacher: What countries have you studied about in Social Studies?
Student: Australia, Asia, Canada, Michigan, and Missouri.

ANIMALS

Mark: We got a puppy!
Teacher: How old is it?
Mark: I don't know. We haven't celebrated its birthday yet.

Teacher: Name a zoo animal.
Roy: A bald-headed eagle.

Jeff: I licked a dog once!

Teacher: Name a farm animal.
Michael: A lamp.

Sharon: I went to the zoo yesterday and saw a big draft!

Teacher: What birds do you see at your house?
Loretta: A regular bird.
Leonard: A red jay!

SCHOOL OPEN HOUSE —TEACHER CONFERENCES

Teacher: I'll be here at school for Parent Conferences Wednesday night.
Jean: My mom won't be here.
Teacher: Why?
Jean: She teaches school.
Teacher: Where?
Jean: I think I forgot.

Teacher: Can your mom come to Parent-Teacher Conferences?
Student: What time?
Teacher: Six to seven PM.
Student: She can come if she's not taking a bath.

Teacher: How was Open House?
Student: Not so good.
Teacher: How could you tell?
Student: By the look on my mother's face.

In social studies we
just finished the chapter
on Israel. Tell me:
what is a "Kibbutz"?

I know: it's the very
last car on a train

FOOD

Sara: Some birds are "poetry."
Teacher: What do you mean by "poetry"?
Sara: You know: they are "poetry." Birds that you can eat!

Teacher: Billy, are you going to plant a garden this year?
Billy: Yes. We're gonna plant salary!

Teacher: What is "soot"?
Student: Isn't it some kind of Chinese food?

Donna: My mom's trying to win a Burger King game.
Teacher: McDonald's just had a contest also.
Donna: Yeah! They coffeed!

Teacher: What dairy food do you like to eat?
Student: College cheese!

Teacher: Joshua, did you eat lots of weenies on your class picnic?
Joshua: Weenies? We didn't eat weenies! We had hot dogs!

Teacher: What do you like for breakfast?
Student: Panty-cakes!
Teacher: Panty-cakes? How do you make "panty cakes"?
Student: From panty-cake mix!

Did you have weenies on tour class picnic?

we didn't have weenies! we had hot dogs!

WRONG WORD

Katrina: My mom told me a lady put her purse on the street and jumped off a high level table.

Teacher: what is your favorite singing group?
Doreen: Gladys Knight and the Pimps!

Teacher: Use "theater" in a sentence.
Student: I know a boy named "Theater."

Teacher: Please put the word "thermometer" in a sentence.
Student: I use a "thermometer" to take my tenchipur.

Teacher: Kim, tell me about The Statue of Liberty.
Kimberly: I read about it in my "Elastic News" magazine.

Teacher: What is a "tepee"?
Student: Something you watch.

Ricky (after falling on the sidewalk): Watch that last step. It's a luau!

Teacher: What is your favorite store?
Ben: How do you spell "Russ"?
Teacher: Why?
Ben: For Toys Are Russ!

Teacher: Where is the rest of our speech group?
Tony: I don't know. Maybe because they're aspirin. You know: not here.

Teacher: Isn't Sandra here today?
Student: No, but I saw her. If she is not at school she stay out and play kookie.

Student: I saw a church staple!

Student: I ran up to my teacher and told her I saw a used condominium on the playground!

Martin: I sleep on a bump bed!

Student: Sorry I am late. I had an accent.

There's nothing like a good lunch. And that's exactly what this is : nothing like a good lunch!

Iss

NAME SOMETHING WITH "YOUR SOUND..."

Teacher: Name an animal with your (s) sound in it.
Peter: A soldier.

Teacher: Edgar, what is your favorite color?
Edgar: Yellow.
Teacher: Why is that?
Edgar: Because it has my (l) sound in it.

Teacher: Tobey, name an animal with your (r) sound in it.
Tobey: Roberta!

Teacher: Name something you can touch that has your (s) sound in it.
Tim: Girls!

Teacher: Name an object with your (th) sound in it.
Student: A spoon of thread.

Teacher: Name a city with your (s) sound.
Student: Down South.

Teacher: What famous men and women have your (s) sound in their name?
Student: John Wayne!

Teacher: Michael, use the word "ring" in a sentence.
Michael: When I get married I'm gonna give my girlfriend a engagement ring.

Teacher: What did you see over Christmas vacation that has your (s) sound in it?
Steven: My sister taking a bath!

Teacher: Matthew: you are working on the (r) sound. Name a country with your (r) in it.
Matthew: Puerto Rico.
Teacher: Very good! Where is Puerto Rico?
Matthew: In Hawaii!

Teacher: Charles, name your favorite animal with your (l) sound.
Charles: My favorite animal is Elizabeth!

Teacher: Billy, name a movie with your (l) sound in the title.
Billy: The Lizard of Oz.

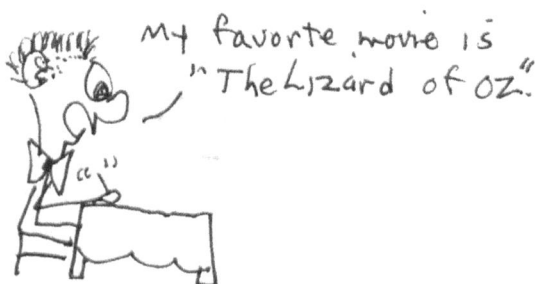

My favorte movie is "The Lizard of Oz."

STATEMENTS FOR ABSOLUTELY NO PARTICULAR REASON AT ALL!

Brandon: I had cherry pie for dessert with cherries in it!

Brian: I'm gonna keep a scrapbook of my tears.

Jonathon (with tears in his eyes): My eyes are melting!

Sam: I'm actually a 42 year-old midget. My mom doesn't know that, so she sends me to school!

David: I don't breathe as well as I used to.

Albert: I'm gonna be here today!

Student (reading a story aloud): "Two women, all of them ladies...."

Robert: Mitch won't be here today. He swallowed a nickel over the weekend.

Sara to Elaine: That's very better!

Akeem: I'm done. Very done.

John: I gotta get my watch fixed: it's twenty-four hours slow.

Ricky: Any boy who wears a skirt is a sissy.....unless he lives in Scotland.

Jeremy: What would anybody do with a butterfly in their soup?

Albert: Have a weekend!

Darryl: Teacher, you remind me of a friend of mine named Carl. He's hyper.

Brittany: Don't write on your mom's face when she's asleep.

Tom: Last night was a bad day!

Matt: we got to go fishing almost.

Francine: I saw a obstacle illusion!

while playing the game "Perquackey" with letter cubes. Joel, working on the (l) sound, was supposed to leave the "L" cube out of the cup and put all the rest of the lettered cubes in the cup. Instead he put all the lettered cubes in the cup including the one with the (l) on it. He thought for a moment, realized he put all the lettered cubes in the cup and said: "I'd better get the (l) outta there!"

In science class I crossed a bee with a door bell and got a "hum dinger!"

"IT MAKES SENSE TO ME!"

Teacher: Who can tell me what is wrong with this picture of a chair?
Jill: The chair don't got no legs.
Teacher: You mean "The chair is missing all its legs."
Jill: Yeah! That's more better!

Teacher: What happened when Samson got his hair cut off?
Student: His strength got weak.

Is that a ground hog or a wood chuck?

Neither. It's a ground chuck!

Teacher: What would you do with a million dollars?
Student: Get a new school!
Teacher: Why?
Student: 'Cause the ceiling is coming down in my classroom upstairs.

Teacher: What makes you happy?
Larry: When my mom and dad don't argue anymore.

Teacher: What would you find in a hobby shop?
Eric: Hobbies!

Steven: I'm not going to be here February, March, April, May, or June.
Teacher: Why not?
Steven: We're moving.
Teacher: Did your father get another job?
Steven: No. He got transferred.

Jeffrey: Know what time I stayed up till last Friday?
Teacher: No. What time?
Jeffrey: 11:57!

Teacher: What did you do yesterday?
Alan: I went to the bathroom a few times.

Matt: (Just after being chosen "Good Citizen of the week" by his classroom teacher) Look at my pea shooter! It's disguised as a pipe.
Teacher: Would a "Citizen of the week" do that?
Matt: Yes. But only after school.

Teacher: Joanie, where is your tooth?
Joanie: I lost it.
Teacher: What did you get when you found it and put it under your pillow?
Joanie: Fifty cents.

Teacher: Do you know what happens when I put my tooth under my pillow?
Freddie: You're too old, teacher, for your teeth to come out.
Damon: My dad's does every night!

Teacher: I like your watch Falisha.
Falisha: It don't work.
Teacher: They why are you wearing it?
Falisha: I like to look at it.

Teacher: Is anyone going anywhere special today?
Jamie: I'm going to the dentist to have a tooth pulled.
Teacher: Why?
Jamie: I have a cavity.
Peggy: Couldn't he pull the cavity instead?

Andy: My tooth came out last night and I put it under my pillow.
Teacher: How much money did you get?
Andy: 250 cents.

Student: Pamela is not here.
Teacher: Is she absent?
Student: No. She's sick.

James: I fell down yesterday and hurt my head.
Teacher: How is your head today?
James: It hurts when I comb my hair.

Warren: My mom lets me play in the rain.
Teacher: Why, Warren?
Warren: So I can get my hair wet and my mom don't have to wash it.

Elain: I'M TIRED!
Teacher: Elain: be quiet. You're too noisy.
Elain: (whispering) I'm tired.

Teacher: Jermaine, do you see your silhouette profile on the chalkboard?
Jermaine: Uh, huh. I see my face too!

Teacher (holding a picture of a clock):
What is this?
Student: A cuckoo clock.
Teacher: I don't think so. I don't see a
cuckoo. Do you?
Student: Then it's a people clock

Student: Teacher, Patti won't be here this
afternoon.
Teacher: Why?
Student: She's absent.
Teacher: You know, maybe I should have
thought of that.
Student: Maybe your brain was asleep.

Teacher: Tired?
Student: No: just sleepy.

Teacher: What do you think makes people
laugh?
Student: Laughing gas!

Teacher: Hi, Jeanette. I had your brother in speech class a few years ago. I probably wouldn't recognize him today.
Jeanette: He looks the same except he's got pimples on his face.

Teacher: What famous birthdays are in February?
Student: Lincoln, Washington, and my sister's.

Teacher: Who was Fredrick Douglas?
Student: He flew the Atlantic alone.

Keith: I just read "Alice In Wonderland."
Teacher: Tell me, Keith, what was the story about?
Keith: "Sleeping Beauty."

Student: Teacher, do you like babies?
Teacher: They're okay. Do you?
Student: No.
Teacher: Why not?
Student: They stink!

Teacher: Robert, what makes you laugh?
Robert: Cynthia.
Teacher: Cynthia, what makes you laugh?
Cynthia: Robert.

Teacher: What is in your mouth, Cathy?
Cathy: A finger nail. It's cherry.
Teacher: What? I don't understand.
Cathy: I put cherry juice on each finger so I can bite my nails in school.

Student: I can't color today.
Teacher: Why not?
Student: My hand is sleepy.

why are those humming birds humming?

Because they don't know the words!

ADVICE I GOT MY VERY FIRST WEEK OF TEACHING FROM "OLD PRO" EDUCATORS:

"I wouldn't mind teaching so much if it wasn't for the children."

From a principal: "Forget everything you ever learned in college!"

ASKING THE TEACHER

Student: Do you have a boy?
Teacher: No.
Student: Do you have a daughter?
Teacher: No. I have two daughters.
Student: Are you married?

Student: Teacher, are you married?
Teacher: No.
Student: Do you have any children?

Student: Teacher, what is your first name?
Teacher: I don't think it would be appropriate if I told you.
Student: We'll give you a dollar.

Teacher: Sorry I am late, class. How long have you been here?

Student: As long as you've been gone.

Oh, no! The door to my lab is gone!

Don't worry. My dog will find it. He's a "lab-door" retriever!